Dracula

and Other Vampire Stories

Eric Kudalis

Capstone Press

MINNEAPOLIS

Printed in the United States of America.

Capstone Press • 2440 Fernbrook Lane • Minneapolis, MN 55447

Editorial Director   John Coughlan
Managing Editor   John Martin
Copy Editor   Theresa Early
Editorial Assistant   Michelle Wood

Library of Congress Cataloging-in-Publication Data

Kudalis, Eric, 1960-
    Dracula and other vampire stories / Eric Kudalis.
        p. cm. -- (Classic monster stories)
    Includes bibliographical references and index.
    Summary: The vampire Dracula pursues his hunger for blood, both in Transylvania and London. Includes information about vampire stories in books and films and the historical background of Dracula.
    ISBN 1-56065-212-8 (lib. bdg.)
    ISBN 1-56065-924-6 (pb.)
    [1. Vampires--Fiction. 2. Vampires.] I. Title. II. Series.
PZ7.K94855Dr   1994
[Fic]--dc20   93-42833
                                                    CIP
                                                    AC

Table of Contents

Chapter 1

The Best-Known Dracula Story

Vampires, the blood-drinking **undead**. They have long been a popular subject for books, plays, and movies. The most famous vampire is Count Dracula. The best-known story about him is told in the classic 1931 movie *Dracula*.

The Story of *Dracula*

The carriage creaked and swayed on the dirt roads through the mountains of Transylvania. Mist began to settle as the sun slipped behind the mountains.

Renfield's journey from England had been long and tiring. He was glad to see the inn. He decided to spend the night there.

"Where are you going?" the innkeeper asked Renfield.

"Castle Dracula," Renfield answered.

The innkeeper gave him a strange look.

"I have business with Count Dracula," Renfield continued. "He wants to buy a piece of property in England."

A Warning about Dracula

The innkeeper's wife warned, "There are vampires there. They live off of the blood of others. Don't go near Castle Dracula."

Renfield thought, vampires do not exist. These villagers are full of **superstitions**.

The next morning, as Renfield prepared to leave, the innkeeper's wife gave him a **crucifix**.

"This will protect you from evil," she told him. Renfield thanked her for the gift. He doubted he would need it.

The Trip to Castle Dracula

The carriage sped through the mountains. When the driver reached Borgo Pass, he stopped abruptly.

"This is as far as I go," he said.

Renfield stood alone at the side of the road. Suddenly another carriage approached. The driver was cloaked in black. The driver motioned for him to get in.

The carriage drove faster and faster. Renfield leaned out the window to caution the driver, but he saw no one. All he saw was a bat flying above the horses, as though it were driving the carriage.

Inside the Castle

The fog was thick as the carriage pulled up to Castle Dracula. Renfield got out.

The dark castle loomed before him. The stone walls were sooty with age. Bats shrieked as they swirled around the turrets.

A door swung open, and Renfield entered the castle. The castle looked abandoned. Walls were cracked. Thick cobwebs hung across doorways.

A bat darted across the entry room. Renfield ducked to avoid it.

"I Am Dracula"

Renfield looked up. He saw a man in black, formal evening clothes coming down the stairs. The man's face was white, as though he hadn't seen the sun in years.

"I am Dracula," he said. "Welcome."

Dracula led Renfield to a clean, well-lit part of the castle. Dracula motioned to a dinner table. "I thought you might be hungry," he said. "Please sit down. Let me offer you some wine."

Renfield asked Dracula if he, too, would have a glass of wine.

Dracula stiffened. "I never drink. . . wine," Dracula said.

Down to Business

After dinner, they sat down to business. Dracula signed the **deeds** to his new property in England. Renfield picked up a letter opener and accidentally cut his finger.

The sight of blood made Dracula's eyes glow. He moved toward Renfield.

As Renfield reached for a napkin, the crucifix hanging around his neck fell into view.

Dracula winced.

"It's only a small cut. Nothing to worry about," Renfield said.

"Oh, yes," Dracula said. "In that case, I bid you good night. Sleep well."

Renfield's Mysterious Visitors

Renfield prepared for bed. He suddenly felt someone else in the room. Renfield turned and saw three women.

They were dressed in flowing gowns. None of them spoke. The women seemed to glide across the floor without taking steps.

A bat darted in front of them. They gazed at the bat, as if they were communicating with it.

Renfield felt dizzy. He fell to the floor.

The bat flew out the window.

Dracula appeared. He knelt by Renfield.

Slowly Dracula spread his black cape, like a bat's wings, and bent over Renfield.

He drove his fangs into Renfield's neck and drank. Renfield now belonged to Dracula. Dracula was ready to set out for England.

To England

The ship tossed about in a storm at sea. Deep in the hull, several coffin-like boxes were addressed to Count Dracula at Carfax **Abbey**.

The boxes held earth from Transylvania. And they held . . . something else.

The storm grew worse. When the ship got to England, the crew were dead. The ship drifted ashore.

The authorities came on board to inspect. They opened a hatch and found Renfield. His eyes looked crazed. He laughed uncontrollably.

"The poor fellow is insane. He's been driven mad by the storm," they said.

They took Renfield to a nearby **sanatorium** run by Dr. Seward. The four earth-filled boxes were delivered to Carfax Abbey, outside London.

Dracula's Neighbors

Dracula went to the theater in London. He asked an usher to lead him to Dr. Seward's.

Dracula introduced himself.

"I just moved here from Transylvania," Dracula told him. "I bought the old abbey next to your property."

Dr. Seward was happy to meet his new neighbor. He introduced Dracula to his daughter,

Mina, her **fiancé**, Jonathan Harker, and Lucy, Mina's childhood friend, who was staying with them.

Dracula stared at Lucy's pale neck.

For days after the meeting, Lucy thought about Dracula. She heard a strange voice calling out to her. She knew it was Count Dracula.

Lucy's Sudden Death

One night a bat flew into Lucy's room. She fell into a trance. Dracula stood above her.

Dracula bent over Lucy and dug his long, sharp fangs into her neck. He sucked until no blood was left.

Dr. Seward was puzzled by Lucy's sudden death. He also was concerned about Renfield, who still acted strangely. He ate flies and laughed all the time.

Dr. Seward decided to send for his friend and former teacher, Professor Van Helsing.

The Blood of a Vampire

Van Helsing examined Lucy's lifeless body. He then drew blood from Renfield.

Lucy in Dracula's clutches

The professor told Dr. Seward, "This is no human blood. This is the blood of a vampire."

Dr. Seward laughed. "Modern science has no room for vampires," he said.

Dreams of a Vampire

After Lucy's funeral, Mina slept poorly. She had nightmares.

She dreamed that a bat flew into her room. She saw a face with burning red eyes. Something bit her on the neck. In the distance, Mina heard the howls of wolves.

When she woke in the morning, she was tired. She felt as though the blood had been drained from her.

As she told Jonathan Harker about her nightmares, Van Helsing stood on the stairs and listened.

He knew that a vampire was on the prowl.

Marks on Mina's Neck

Van Helsing asked to see Mina's neck. Mina reluctantly opened her collar.

Just as Van Helsing suspected, there were two red marks on Mina's neck.

"Where did these marks come from?" Van Helsing asked.

Before Mina could answer, Count Dracula appeared at the door.

Dracula had come to pay a visit.

"Count Dracula, I want to show you something," Van Helsing said. "Look at this cigarette box."

Van Helsing opened the box suddenly. Dracula jumped back. He knocked the box to the floor.

A mirror was on the inside lid. Van Helsing knew that vampires cast no reflections in mirrors. Now Van Helsing had proof that Dracula was, indeed, a vampire.

To Destroy Dracula

"I am so sorry," Dracula said to Dr. Seward. "I do not like mirrors."

Dracula turned to Van Helsing. "You have not

Dracula jumps back after Professor Van Helsing opens the cigarette box.

lived an entire lifetime," he said, "but you are a very wise man."

With that, Dracula left.

Van Helsing knew his next task. Dracula had to be destroyed before he turned more people into vampires.

As the days passed, Mina could not get her mind off Dracula. At night she heard something calling to her.

Professor Van Helsing told Mina's nurse to drape garlic cloves around her bed. They would ward off the vampire.

Dracula's Silent Call

In the cellar of the abbey, Dracula slept in his coffin. He slowly lifted the lid and rose from his coffin. Without speaking a word, he called to Mina.

Mina heard Dracula's silent cry. She brushed the garlic aside and rose from her bed. She slipped out an open window. She walked in a **trance** toward Dracula's abbey.

When the nurse came into the bedroom to check on Mina, she screamed. "She's gone, she's gone!"

Professor Van Helsing rushed into the bedroom with Jonathan Harker and Dr. Seward.

"She's gone to Dracula," Van Helsing cried. He grabbed a wooden **stake**. "We must hurry to the abbey."

The Rush to Save Mina

At the abbey, they searched every room. The abbey was as silent and musty as a tomb.

Soon the sun would rise. They knew Dracula had to return to his coffin or the sun would kill him.

They found two coffins lying side by side. They feared Mina was in one, already a vampire. But the first one was empty. Van Helsing opened the other.

The three men stood in amazement. Dracula lay in the coffin.

"I need something to pound the stake through Dracula's heart," Van Helsing told Jonathan.

Jonathan saw a figure in white standing in the shadows.

"Mina," he called out.

Mina pulled back.

Van Helsing couldn't wait. He found a large rock and aimed it above the wooden stake.

Death of Dracula

With a swift blow, Van Helsing drove the stake through Dracula's heart.

Dracula howled like an animal caught in a trap. He clutched at the stake as blood spurted from the wound.

Mina began to scream, as though she, too, could feel Dracula's pain.

With one last cry, Dracula released his grip.

Mina felt a great release. She fell backward and Jonathan caught her. Mina was free from Dracula's power.

The evil Count Dracula lay dead in his coffin, never to roam the night again.

Bram Stoker, the author of the original Dracula story.

Chapter 2
Bram Stoker

The story of Dracula is based on a book by Bram Stoker. *Dracula* was published in 1897.

Nearly 100 years later, the book is still read by many people. And Stoker's story is enjoyed by millions on television and film.

Stoker was born in Dublin, Ireland, in 1847. He was a manager for an actor. He also wrote for magazines and newspapers for extra money.

Stoker first heard about the vampires of Eastern Europe from a professor friend at the University of Budapest in Hungary. Stoker began to collect tales of vampires.

Chapter 3

Superstitions about Vampires

Vampire legends were especially popular in areas around Transylvania during the 1500s and 1600s. There are also stories of vampires from ancient Greece, Egypt, and China.

The "Undead"

According to these stories, vampires are cursed. They were once alive but now exist in the world of the "undead." They are both dead and alive. They are not welcome among either the living or the dead. So they roam the earth.

Vampires are believed to exist for centuries. Many of them, like Dracula, become very wealthy during their long lives.

Feeding on the Blood of the Living

The legends say that vampires rise from their graves and prowl at night. They feed on the blood of the living. If a vampire sucks all of a victim's blood, the victim also becomes one of the undead.

Vampires sleep in their original graves or in coffins filled with dirt from their homeland. They fear the sun. It could kill them, or, at the very least, make them weak.

In some stories, vampires can change themselves into bats.

Keeping Vampires Away

Keeping a vampire away is difficult. Crosses, **holy water**, and religious objects are used to ward off vampires. Plants such as wolfsbane and petals of wild roses are also said to be effective.

If you hang bulbs of garlic on your bed or

drape them around your neck you can sleep soundly. But garlic will not kill a vampire.

How to Kill a Vampire

In some superstitions, to kill a vampire you must drive a wooden stake through its heart.

In many stories, the vampire-killer follows the creature to its grave. When the vampire is asleep, the hunter pries open the coffin. With a swift swing, the vampire-killer drives the stake into the vampire's heart. In some tales, the hunter must also cut off the vampire's head and even burn the body.

Despite their screams of agony, vampires are grateful to those who kill them. Death means peace for them at last.

A 15th century woodcut of "Vlad the Impaler"

Chapter 4

The Real Dracula

In writing *Dracula,* Bram Stoker wove fact with fiction. He studied the vampire **legends** of Eastern Europe. But his greatest inspiration came from history.

The true stories of two cruel rulers found their way into Stoker's story. These rulers were Vlad Dracula, known by historians as "Vlad the Impaler," and Countess Elizabeth Bathory.

Vlad the Impaler

Vlad Dracula was born in 1431. He ruled Wallachia, in what is now Romania, from 1456 to 1462. Wallachia is now part of Romania.

Vlad's evil deeds are well known. Some historians blame him for nearly 100,000 deaths. His favorite method of killing was to **impale** his victims with a long, sharp pole.

Eating a Meal among the Corpses

In 1459, Vlad Dracula impaled several thousand Germans. He then sat down to eat, with the bloodied victims hanging on poles all around him.

Vlad murdered Bulgars, Hungarians, Germans, Turks, Gypsies, Jews, and his own people as well. Impaling was his favorite method of killing, but he also burned people alive, pounded nails through their heads, and chopped them to pieces.

In 1462, Vlad fled north when the Turks stormed his castle. He was captured by the Hungarians. He was finally released and died in battle in 1476.

Stories of Vlad the Impaler haunted the countryside for centuries. Some people even reported seeing him 200 years after his death.

Countess Elizabeth Bathory

Vlad the Impaler did not actually drink his victims' blood. Countess Elizabeth Bathory did.

Born in 1560, Elizabeth Bathory also lived in Transylvania. Her story is particularly gruesome.

Bathing in Blood

Countess Bathory became obsessed with youth and beauty. She thought that the blood of young girls would keep her young. With the help of her servants, the countess **lured** girls to her castle. She sliced them open and then bathed in their blood.

Some think she killed as few as 50 girls. Others estimate she had more than 600 victims. Tales of her horrible deeds spread. In 1610, villagers finally seized the castle.

Countess Bathory was tried for murder. Her assistants were **executed**. Because she was royalty, the countess could not be executed. Instead, she was walled up in a tiny room in her castle. There she died in 1614.

A scene from Francis Ford Coppola's *Bram Stoker's Dracula*, 1992

Chapter 5

Vampires in Books and Film

Bram Stoker's *Dracula* is the most famous vampire story, but it is only one of many.

The physician Dr. John Polidori wrote *The Vampyre* in 1819.

A vampire opera was performed in Germany in 1828. In 1851 the French writer Alexandre Dumas wrote a vampire drama.

Even now, authors are fascinated by vampires. Anne Rice's *Interview with the Vampire,* published in 1976, is a modern vampire legend.

The First Vampire Movie

The first vampire movie was a 1922 German production called *Nosferatu,* directed by F.W. Murnau.

In *Nosferatu,* Dracula is called Count Orlock. Count Orlock is one of the most frightening vampires ever portrayed in movies. He is completely bald and has pointed ears, sharp teeth, and long, crooked fingers.

In 1927, John Balderston and Hamilton Deane wrote a stage version of *Dracula.* Bela Lugosi starred in the play.

Other Vampire Films

This play was made into a movie by director Tod Browning in 1931. Bela

Count Orlock

Lugosi also starred in this film. Browning's *Dracula* is still the most famous of the many vampire films.

The vampire-movie craze continues to this day. Bela Lugosi starred in *The Mark of the Vampire* (1935) and *The Return of the Vampire* (1944). Lugosi became known worldwide as Dracula.

The Mark of the Vampire, 1935

Two other famous vampire films were *Dracula's Daughter* (1936) and *Son of Dracula* (1943).

Bud Abbott and Lou Costello even filmed a comic Dracula. In *Abbott and Costello Meet Frankenstein* (1948), the two main characters try to escape Frankenstein, Dracula, and the Wolf Man.

Grandpa and Herman in "The Munsters."

Television Vampires

In the 1960s, television audiences got a taste of vampire humor with the series "The Munsters." The vampire was a lovable "grandpa" who was always fumbling about in his **dungeon** laboratory.

Vampires in Color

The vampire films of the 1930s and 1940s

were filmed in black and white. In the 1950s, Dracula took on a new look in color.

Hammer Studios in England produced *The Horror of Dracula* (1957). This film starred Christopher Lee. His Dracula had burning, red eyes and blood-dripping fangs.

The Horror of Dracula used new film technology. The final scene, for instance, shows Dracula slowly turning to dust in the sunlight.

A lobby card from the Universal Studios movie, *Dracula*.

Gary Oldman as Dracula

Dracula in the 1990s

Directed by Francis Ford Coppola in 1992, *Bram Stoker's Dracula* starred Gary Oldman as Dracula and Anthony Hopkins as Dr. Van Helsing. This film followed Bram Stoker's book very closely.

Chapter 6

Vampire Bats

Although human vampires are the stuff of legend, vampire bats are the real thing.

Vampire bats live in Central and South America. They are about the size of a mouse.

They are called vampire bats because they live off the blood of animals, mostly cattle. They bite into the animal and then suck blood.

Vampire bats are harmless. Because they are so small, vampire bats cannot suck much blood from the animals they bite. In

fact, they do not harm them at all. The bat gets
its nutrition from the animal's blood.

They do not bite humans or drink human

blood. Like other bats, they avoid people. Like all bats, vampire bats are active at night.

Glossary

abbey–a building where monks or holy men once lived

crucifix–a figure of Christ on the cross

deed–legal paper showing ownership

dungeon–a dark prison or room, usually underground

executed–killed by the government as punishment

fiancé–a man engaged to marry a woman

holy water–water that has been blessed by a priest

impale–to stab with a long, sharp stick

legend–an old story

lure–to draw into danger by offering a seeming reward

sanatorium–a specialized hospital

stake–a sharpened stick

superstitious–believing in magic, luck, or legends

trance–a state of being deeply unaware of one's surroundings or events; being focused only on something other than the world nearby

undead–a person killed by a vampire but not allowed to be dead

vampire–an "undead" person in old stories who is supposed to suck the blood of living people

To Learn More

About Dracula in the movies:

Cohen, Daniel. *Masters of Horror.* New York: Clarion Books, 1984.

Powers, Tom. *Horror Movies.* Minneapolis: Lerner Publications Company, 1989.

Thorne, Ian. *Dracula.* Mankato, MN: Crestwood House, 1977.

About bats:

Johnson, Sylvia. *Bats.* Minneapolis: Lerner Publications Company, 1985.

Pringle, Laurence. *Vampire Bats.* New York: Morrow, 1982.

Shebar, Sharon Sigmond, and Susan E. Shebar. *Bats.* New York: Franklin Watts, 1990.

About Romania:

Carran, Betty B. *Romania.* Chicago: Childrens Press, 1992.

Stewart, Gail B. *Romania.* New York: Crestwood House, 1991.

Index

Photo Credits:
Hollywood Book and Poster: cover, pp. 4, 9, 13, 15, 18, 22, 24; Archive Photos: pp. 10, 32, 34, 35, 36, 37, 38; Merlin D. Tuttle: pp. 40, 41, 42-43.